Sparkle World Annual 2013

Sparkle World Annual 2013

All of this inside...

RAINBOW magic

Barbie™

MY LITTLE PONY

Littlest Pet Shop

Puppy in my Pocket

polly pocket

The Goblin Princess

Stories

Colour

Crafts & Recipes

Group Editor: Anita Cash.
Editorial and design assistants: Louise Fell, Emma Dyson and Kate Farrell.

Sparkle World® Annual 2013 is published by Redan Publishing Limited, Shrewsbury, SY3 7NR and distributed by DC Thomson Annuals Limited. **Sparkle World**® logo and **Redan** logo are trademarks of Redanco Ltd. **Adventures in Pocketville** © 2012 MEG and Giochi Preziosi S.P.A. Puppy In My Pocket® and Pocketville® are registered trademarks of MEG CUCCIOLI CERCA AMICI® is a registered trademark of Giochi Preziosi All rights reserved. **Barbie** ©2012 Mattel Inc. All rights reserved. **Littlest Pet Shop** ©2012 Hasbro. All rights reserved. Licensed by Hasbro. **My Little Pony** ©2012 Hasbro. All Rights Reserved. Licensed by Hasbro. **Polly Pocket** and associated trademarks are owned by Mattel, Inc., and used under license from Mattel Europa, B.V. ©2012 Mattel, Inc. All Rights Reserved. **Puppy In My Pocket**® ©2012 MEG; Puppy In My Pocket® is a registered trademarks of MEG. All Rights Reserved. Licensed by Licensing Works!®. **Rainbow Magic** ©2012 Rainbow Magic Limited. **Strawberry Shortcake**™ ©2012 Those Characters from Cleveland, Inc. Used under license by Redan Publishing Limited. **The Goblin Princess**® is a registered trademark and copyright © 2012 Redanco Ltd. All rights reserved. **YooHoo and Friends** © Aurora World Corp.

Redan Publishing is working to ensure that all its paper is produced without the use of chlorine and is sourced from well-managed forests (along the lines laid down by the Forest Stewardship Council).

Redan

Activities

10 Help Barbie and her sisters work out these doll-lightful puzzles!

12 Find out what kind of animal Tiki is!

14 Who is your fabtastic best friend?

18 Help Kate and Magic through the maze to the palace.

22 Help the pets spot the differences between the pictures.

31 Reveal Sky's secret by solving the Rainbow Magic code!

32 YooHoo has a look and find activity for you.

40 YooHoo and Pammee are flying over Yootopia.

42 What's your pet personality? Find out in this quiz!

44 Help the Puppy In My Pocket puppies solve these puzzles!

48 This part is all about YOU! Just fill in the gaps.

50 Help Strawberry with her berry big wordsearch!

58 Which of Strawberry's exciting adventures would suit you best?

64 Discover what your popstar name is with Barbie.

70 Guide Twilight Sparkle to Pinkie Pie's party!

72 Solve the number trail to help Strawberry get to the dance studio.

75 Polly's got some poptastic jokes to make you giggle!

78 Help the fairies spot the differences between the pictures!

82 Find out your friendship score with YooHoo's quiz!

86 Choose and design a gorgeous outfit for Barbie!

90 Help the Puppy In My Pocket puppies solve the wordsearch.

Games

28 Go bingo crazy with the ponies!

52 Test your memory with Polar Bear's game!

62 Play this funtastic game with Polly Pocket and her friends!

88 Play this Strawberry Shortcake game, collecting fruit along the way.

Puppy in my Pocket
Adventures in Pocketville

YooHoo & FRIENDS
© Aurora World Corp.

Strawberry Shortcake

Hello, Sparklets! Welcome to this sparkletastic Sparkle World Annual 2013! We've had lots of fun putting it together and it's bursting with sparkly things just for you. Don't forget to log on to our website, www.mysparkleworld.com for chances to win prizes and lots more activities and fun!

Sparkly kisses!
The Sparkle Girls xXx

Em Lou Helen Jazz

Totally sparkly!

www.mysparkleworld.com

This super sparkly **Sparkle World** annual belongs to

·······································
·······································

Write your name here.

THE HERO OF PONYVILLE!

Apple Blossom, Scootaloo and Sweetie Belle need help!

Help! We're going to fall!

1 It was a quiet day in the little town of Ponyville. Rainbow Dash was cruising through the sky when suddenly she heard cries from the pony treehouse below! "Help! Help!" shouted Apple Blossom, Scootaloo and Sweetie Belle. "Oh, no!" gasped Rainbow Dash. "The treehouse is going to fall!" She zoomed into action at once!

That was so awesome!

Wow! I have a fan club!

2 Rainbow Dash quickly carried the three little ponies to safety, just in time. The treehouse crashed to the ground! "You're our hero!" squealed Apple Blossom.

3 "Rainbow Dash, you're so cool!" called Scootaloo, as they watched her fly off. "I want to be like her when I'm big." Apple Blossom agreed, "From now on we're the official Rainbow Dash fan club!"

♥ 4 Rainbow Dash didn't want to disappoint her fans. She zoomed around Ponyville at superspeed looking for more ponies to help. "Uh-oh, that lightning just set Applejack's house on fire!" she cried.

Great job, Rainbow Dash!

Never fear, Rainbow Dash is here!

♥ 5 She raced to the rescue with a bucket of water and soon put it out! "Thank you, Rainbow Dash," said Applejack. "You saved my house." "No problem!" grinned Rainbow Dash. "It's all part of a hero's job!"

I saved Applejack's whole house! By myself!

♥ 6 Afterwards, Rainbow Dash told her Fan Club all about how she saved the ponies from the treehouse and how she saved the house from fire. "Wow, you're the most awesome pony in town!" grinned Sweetie Belle. "It's a good job I was there," grinned Rainbow Dash. "Hmm!" Applejack told her pony friends later on. "Rainbow Dash has a kind heart, but I think she's getting a bit too big for her horseshoes!"

7 Later, Rainbow Dash heard cries for help. She dashed to find out what was going on and spotted Twilight Sparkle. "Spike brushed against a magic plant and it turned him into a giant baby dragon!" Twilight Sparkle told her. "I have a cure, but he's having fun and won't let me use it!" "Ha! Just leave it to me," said Rainbow Dash.

8 She found Spike wasn't only a giant dragon. He had a giant appetite too! And he was eating everything in town! "Okay, put the cupcakes down and come quietly," Rainbow Dash ordered Spike.

9 But Spike took no notice! Fluttershy flew up and tapped Rainbow Dash on the shoulder. "Can I help?" she said. "Yes, you're the animal expert, Fluttershy," agreed Rainbow Dash.

At home, Twilight Sparkle bathed Spike with the magic cure and he shrank to normal size. "Thank you, Fluttershy," smiled Twilight Sparkle. "Your skill with animals saved the town!"

10 "Spike, you should know better than to eat all the food in town," scolded Fluttershy, giving him a stare and wagging her hoof. "What do you have to say for yourself?" "S-sorry," said Spike.

12 "And thank you too, Rainbow Dash," added Twilight Sparkle, with a smile. "It's great to be good at something, but it's important to let others shine too. Everyone has their own talent and you remembered that!" "I guess Ponyville is big enough for two heroes!" grinned Rainbow Dash. "After all, I will need a day off every now and again!" All of the ponies laughed. "Neigh! Hey! Hey!"

Barbie Pinktastic Puzzles!

Help Barbie and her sisters work out these doll-lightful puzzles!

Read the sentences below and colour T for true or F for false.

1. Barbie has long blond hair. **T** **F**

2. Chelsea is holding a cat. **T** **F**

3. Skipper has red streaks in her hair. **T** **F**

4. The puppies have white fur. **T** **F**

5. Stacie is wearing a skirt. **T** **F**

Spot 6 differences between pictures A and B. Put a tick in each paw print as you find them.

A

B

There are twelve words hidden in this wordsearch. Draw a line through each one when you find it on the grid. Look carefully because words may appear across, down and diagonal.

BARBIE
GLITTER
SHOES
HANDBAG
CHELSEA
BELT
SUNGLASSES
SKIPPER
BOOTS
STACIE
SKIRT
BRACELET

S	U	N	G	L	A	S	S	E	S
B	C	H	E	L	S	E	A	B	K
O	S	T	A	C	I	E	R	E	I
O	H	E	A	N	R	T	B	L	P
T	O	L	D	I	D	A	T	T	P
S	E	A	B	A	R	B	I	E	E
A	S	K	I	R	T	C	A	B	R
B	R	A	C	E	L	E	T	G	S

Finish the puzzle by drawing the missing jewels in the empty boxes. Each jewel can appear once in each 3 x 3 grid and once in each row or column.

Starting with the letter F, going clockwise around the hearts, write every other letter in the hearts below to reveal what Barbie and her sisters had for breakfast.

Start

Look carefully at the pictures below. Draw a circle around the odd one out.

the Barbie beat

Answers: True or False: 1. True, 2. True, 3. False, 4. False, 5. False. Word wheel: Barbie and her sisters had fruit salad for breakfast. Spot the Differences: 1. There are jewels missing on the left pink jacket hood. 2. The right dog's jacket has changed to purple. 3. The left dog's eyes have changed colour. 4. The right dog's boot is missing. 5. The right dog's tail has changed position. 6. The left dog's boot straps have changed colour.

YooHoo & Friends™
© Aurora World Corp.

Whoo are you?

YooHoo has a friend for you to discover! Find out what kind of animal Tiki is by writing a letter in each shape to make two words.

chim ⬡ ets

schoo ⬡ eap

zebr ⬡ pple

deser ⬡ reat

hone ⬡ awn

was ⬡ aint

tof ⬡ mbrella

cros ⬡ hine

Tiki

___ ___ ___ ___ ___ ___ ___ ___ ___ ___ ___

Write your answer on the lines.

How Many?

Write your answer in the box.

Cute Colouring!

Colour in Flamingo and Hamster using the small picture to help you.

How many flowers can you count?

Write the answer in the box.

Who's your Fabtastic Best Friend?

Answer the questions and follow the arrows to reveal who would be your best friend!

Start
Do you love going on adventures?

Do you love listening to music?

Are you good at keeping secrets?

Do you get up early in the mornings?

Do you have a vivid imagination?

Do you have a large group of friends?

Are you always busy?

Are you a confident person?

Lea

Lea and you would be BFFs! You both have lots of energy and are always planning fab adventures. You are very imaginative and always make sure your friends have a great time!

Polly

You and Polly would be best friends! You always know what's cool and love listening to music. You always put your friends first and never leave anyone out!

Sparkle World Quiz

Do you read a lot of books?

Do you enjoy making new friends?

Do you keep up to date with the latest fashions?

Are you always organising things for you and your friends to do?

Are you always telling your friends jokes?

Is dancing your favourite thing to do at a party?

Are you a good listener?

Do you enjoy baking cakes for your friends?

Are you good at giving advice?

Do you like singing along to your favourite tunes?

Do you like surprises?

Crissy

Crissy and you would be perfect pals. You are both super stylish and love to travel. You are always making new friends and are great at giving your friends advice!

Kerstie

Kerstie and you would be best friends! You are always singing and making your friends laugh. You are bubbly and your friends love to be around you!

RAINBOW magic®

Adele the Singing Coach Fairy

Kirsty and Rachel were friends with the fairies and often helped them when Jack Frost's goblins caused trouble. The two girls were enjoying a picnic at Rainspell Island Music Festival when, suddenly, Adele the Singing Coach Fairy shot out of the hamper in a burst of sparkles!

"The goblins have stolen my magical musical clef," cried Adele. "All the pop stars at the festival will be singing off-key if I don't find it – and fast!"

"We're about to go and watch A-OK rehearse," said Kirsty. "We'll keep an eye out for goblins."

Adele hid inside Rachel's backpack and the girls hurried through the crowd to A-OK's rehearsal tent. The four members of A-OK – Jez, Amir, Rio and Finn – were around the piano, with Alto Adams, their singing coach. The boys began singing but their voices sounded harsh and off-key.

"Terrible!" groaned Alto. Just then, Rio saw Kirsty and Rachel waiting patiently.

"We're not usually this bad," he sighed.

"Could we have your autographs?" asked Rachel.

The four boys gathered around and signed the girls' autograph books. At that moment, a clear beautiful voice sounded out of nowhere!

"I'd climb the highest mountain, just to be with you..."

Rachel and Kirsty could hardly believe their eyes when Gobby, one of the goblins, came out from behind the piano!

"Your singing is wonderful!" cried Alto.

"So can I join the band?" Gobby asked eagerly.

"Of course!" agreed Alto.

"Hurrah!" Gobby yelled, jumping up and down. Kirsty noticed a necklace fly out of his hoodie. It was Adele's magical clef!

"That's why he can sing so well," she whispered to Rachel. Quietly, the girls slipped out.

"I have an idea how to get your clef back," Rachel told Adele.

"Can you change me and Kirsty into fairies?" She explained her plan. With a wave of her wand, Adele transformed the girls into fairies with gossamer wings. The fairies zoomed to A-OK's trailer and slipped inside.

Adele flicked her wand and conjured up a stage outfit and a copy of the clef necklace.

"Now where's Gobby?" said Rachel.

The fairies flew outside and found the A-OK boys and Gobby chatting to fans. Adele returned the girls to human-size then they went up to Gobby.

"Please will you sing for us?" asked Kirsty. Looking pleased with himself, Gobby began to sing. He sang beautifully, but Rachel and Kirsty clapped their hands over their ears.

"You sound awful!" Kirsty told him. "Maybe you're nervous about the concert," added Rachel. "Why not try out your stage outfit?"

"Maybe I should," agreed Gobby, worried. The girls went with him to the trailer. As he admired his outfit he noticed the copy of the clef necklace! Quickly, Kirsty picked it up and tried it on.

"That necklace makes you look like a star," Rachel chimed. "Why don't you try singing?"

"OK!" agreed Kirsty. She sounded terrible, but Rachel cheered and clapped.

"I never realised you had such a great voice!" Rachel declared.

Gobby was now looking very confused.

"I want THAT necklace!" he announced. "This one doesn't work any more!"

He pulled off Adele's necklace and threw it down.

Instantly, Adele zoomed out of Rachel's backpack and caught the necklace!

"Thank you, girls!" she smiled.

"It's a fairy trick," yelled Gobby, stomping away.

As the girls left, they saw the A-OK boys coming towards them.

"We were practising our songs and our singing voices just came back," grinned Finn.

"It was just like magic!" Jez added.

Rachel and Kirsty laughed. The A-OK boys had no idea just how right they were!

Pocketville maze!

Puppy in my Pocket

Adventures in Pocketville

Start

Kate & Magic

Copper

Mela

Colour in the correct heart when you find each character.

Using your finger, or a pencil, help Kate and Magic collect the Pocketville pets in the maze and take them to meet Princess Ava at the palace.

Sparkle World maze

Dot

How many?

Write your answer in the box.

Goldie

Finish Ava

Strawberry Shortcake™

Berry Colourful!

Use your crayons to colour in this rocking picture of Strawberry Shortcake and her friends, using the small picture to help you choose your colours.

Which pet is playing the keyboard?

Custard ☐   Pupcake ☐

Tick the correct box.

Spot the Differences!

Look carefully at the two pictures below. Can you find 8 differences between them? Circle the differences in picture B as you find them.

How many purple paw prints can you count?

Write the answer in the box.

Circle the odd one out.

A   B   C

Can you spot the beach ball?

B

BANANA BONANZA!

POPCORN
FRESH   HOT!

WIN A PR...

Answers – no peeking!

Answers: 1. A ball has appeared next to Hamster. 2. The word 'Fun' has disappeared from the kiosk on the right. 3. The hot dogs sign has changed to say 'Banana Bonanza'. 4. Cat's balloon is now orange. 5. The sun is missing. 6. Flamingo has replaced Monkey 7. One of Ladybird's antennae is missing. 8. Hamster's eyes are now blue. Odd one out answer: B.

Sparkle World crafts & recipes!

Have your own sparkle show!
Make a Puppet Theatre!

You will need:

A large cardboard box
(with flaps!)
Brightly coloured paints
1/2 metre velveteen fabric
Sparkly ribbon/trim
Safety scissors
PVA Glue
An adult to help you!

1. Turn your box on its side and paint it a nice bright colour inside and out. Paint the floor a dark brown colour just like a real stage!

2. Ask an adult to cut a slot each side of the box to slide the puppets through. Cut out curtains from the fabric and trim with sparkly ribbon. Glue them to the side flaps of the box.

3. Draw some floorboards on your stage with a felt-tip pen. Draw or paint a scene for your theatre and glue into place. Download some scenery from www.mysparkleworld.com!

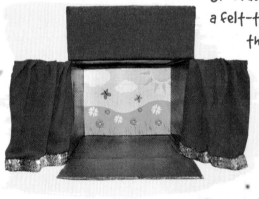

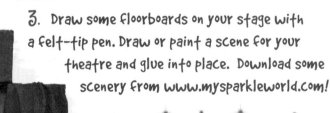

The Sparkle Theatre

4. Decorate the flap at the top to create a sign for your theatre. Fold a piece of fabric like a fan, then drape over the top of the stage to create a theatrical look!

Let's put on a Puppet Show!

Dress up with your friends in your finest theatre clothes!

Sparkle Productions Present
The Sparkle Theatre

To: ....
You're invited to ....'s
Puppet Show!
★ Place: ....
Date: ....
Time: ....

We used sparkly gems to decorate our puppet fairies' wands!

Get creative with making invitations, posters and scenery!

Try acting out some of your favourite Sparkle World stories in your puppet theatre!

Let's make Crunchy Caramel Popcorn!

1. Ask an adult to help you. Combine 250g of caster sugar and 250g of butter together in a saucepan over a moderate heat and cook until caramelised.

2. Remove from the heat and leave to cool.

3. Add 250g of cream very slowly to the mixture, whisking constantly.

4. Pour the mixture into a saucepan and simmer until the cream has thickened slightly.

5. Leave to cool, pour over some ready-made popcorn and serve immediately.

Let's make Puppets!

1. Draw your own puppet characters on to card using coloured pencils or felt-tip pens. Ask an adult to help you cut them out. You can also download some puppet characters from our website!

2. Use sticky tape to attach a lolly stick to the back of your puppets. You can then slide your puppets through the slots on the side of your Sparkle theatre so they can perform in your puppet show!

Download Puppet Theatre invitations, posters and scenery cut-outs from our fab Sparkle World website!

www.mysparkleworld.com

Double Trouble!

Read the story.
When you see a
picture, say the
word instead.

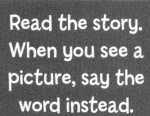

Beagle Twins

ball

Eleanor

 and her were playing on the  when bounded up with her .

"Can you watch my pups while I go for a run?" asked . "Okay," smiled . "Two more won't be any trouble." gave the and the a to play with. The pups had a great time chasing the , especially when it landed in a muddy puddle!

They all dived in after the and got covered in mud from nose to tail! A little later, came back. "Thank you for watching them, ," said . "Come along, pups." When and her had gone, looked at her muddy and smiled, "I think you need a bath!" and the pups nodded in agreement.

 took the  to the nursery and gave them a good scrub. But, once the mud came off  gasped in surprise. They weren't her  at all. They were the ! "Hey, you tricked us!" laughed . The  rolled over on their backs, laughing! Just then,  came back with the real . She had just found out the trick too! "I think I was wrong," chuckled . "Two more are double the trouble!" "Yes, but they're double the fun too!" laughed .

Twice as many puppies really are double the trouble!

LET'S PLAY PONY BINGO!

Pinkie Pie

Princess Celestia

You will need: Two, three or four players, pens, and two dice. How to play: Each player chooses to play with Pinkie Pie, Princess Celestia, Twilight Sparkle or Applejack. Take it in turns to roll the dice and add up the total. Check which picture matches the number thrown. If a player has the same picture, she should cross it out. The winner is the first player to cross out all of their pictures and shout "BINGO!"

TWILIGHT SPARKLE

APPLEJACK

How many?

Write your answer in the box.

RAINBOW magic®

Magical Code!

Sparkle World PUZZLE

Going clockwise from the letter D, write every other letter on the dotted lines below to reveal Sky's secret question!

Start

D_ _ _ _ _ _

_ _ _ _ _ _ _ _ _ _

_ _ _ _ _ _ _ _?

What is your answer to Sky's question?
Colour a flower next to your answer.

yes   no

YooHoo & FRIENDS™
© Aurora World Corp.

Look and find!

Pammee is having a party with her friends! Join in the fun by completing the activities around the page.

Help YooHoo draw lines to match each close-up to where it fits in the big picture.

Who is holding a bunch of pink flowers?
Colour the correct heart.

How many?

Write the numbers in the boxes.

Colour the star when you find the magic green seed.

Sparkle World LOOK

Tick a box next to each thing you find in the picture above.

Y&F

Sparkle World crafts & recipes!

You will need:

- 1 sponge cake
- 1 ready-made tub of vanilla icing/frosting
- 1 bag of white chocolate melts
- 1 bag of pink melts
- cake pop sticks
- edible decorations
- An adult to help you

Let's make CAKE POPS!

A Parent and Child Activity

1 Crumble the sponge cake into a mixing bowl until it looks like fine breadcrumbs. Stir in the icing using a wooden spoon.

2 Using your hands, mould the dough into a large ball and place in the fridge for 30 minutes. Remove the dough from the fridge, break off small pieces and roll them into balls. Put these back in the fridge for a further 10 minutes then remove.

3 Ask an adult to help you melt some of the white chocolate melts in the microwave. Dip the end of a cake pop stick into the chocolate, then put the stick into the middle of a cake ball. Make sure you push them in quite far so that they stay in place.

4 Once they have set, you can decorate your cake pops. Dip your cake pops in pink or white chocolate melts then use your edible decorations to create swirls and pretty patterns!

The Goblin Princess

A Surprise for Smoky!

Gelza, the goblin princess, dislikes anything pretty, pink or cute - except her pet dragon, Smoky!

1 "Mum, have you got a good memory?" asked Gelza one day. "I'm afraid not, my little rabbit dropping," replied the goblin queen. Gelza sighed. "I'm trying to remember when Smoky's hatching day is," she explained. She knew it was sometime soon.

2 Gelza went to the slug patch to ask her dad if he knew. "Do you know when Smoky's hatching day is?" Gelza asked the king. He stopped working and scratched his head. "I'm not sure. Perhaps Mrs Dollop will know," he suggested.

3 "No, my ploppet, I can't remember when little Smoky hatched out," Mrs Dollop told Gelza, "...but I can soon find out!" She hurried away, leaving Gelza rather puzzled and returned after a few moments with a battered old book. "Every night before I go to sleep, I write about my day in this diary," explained Mrs Dollop.

4 "Well I never!" exclaimed Mrs Dollop after searching back through the pages. "It will be three years ago tomorrow!" Gelza was very excited. "Let's give Smoky a hatching day surprise," she said.

5 Gelza and Mrs Dollop set to work right away. Gelza went back out to the king's slug patch to gather slugs and bugs for pizza toppings while Mrs Dollop baked a special hatching day cake, carefully stirring in broken eggshells for added crunch. "Now we just need to think of a party game to play," said Mrs Dollop, when they had finished.

6 Gelza thought hard but wasn't sure what a three year old dragon might like to play. "Why don't we have another look at my diary?" suggested Mrs Dollop. "Here we are..." Mrs Dollop read out what she had written on the day of Gelza's third birthday, "...Gelza had lots of fun playing on a slime slide!"

7 The next day Gelza gave Smoky her wonderful hatching day surprise and everybody joined in the fun. "Wheee!" shouted Gelza, gleefully. "Slime slides are the best fun ever!" Smoky had a wonderful time and Gelza felt very proud of her little dragon. "I want to remember this day forever," she thought.

8 That night, before she went to sleep, Gelza started writing a diary of her own and her first entry was all about Smoky's hatching day surprise!

Retriever Family!

Colour the picture using the small picture to help you.

Eleanor

Lenny

Maxwell

How many?

Write the numbers in the boxes.

YooHoo & FRIENDS™

© Aurora World Corp.

Flying High!

YooHoo and Pammee are having a fun day flying over Yootopia. Using your finger, or a pencil, help Pammee and YooHoo find a path through the clouds to reach Chewoo.

Start

Finish

What's your Pet Personality?

Which two paw prints are you most drawn to?

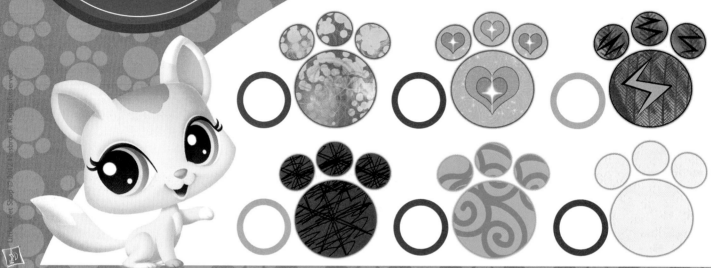

Draw circles around the four descriptions that are most similar to you.

I have lots of friends.

I like exploring new places.

I write secrets in a diary.

I love playing in the park.

I have lots of different hobbies.

I like to try new things.

I am good at giving advice.

I like to give my friends presents.

I love to draw and paint.

What's your pet personality? Tick the answers in each group that you like best, then look at the side bar to find out which pet is your personality icon!

Put a tick next to your 2 favourite objects.

Your pet personality is MOUSE! You are thoughtful, kind and girly. Just like Mouse, you always think of others before thinking of yourself. You are a great person to be around and an excellent friend.

Where is your favourite place?

Theme park

Park

Mostly purple

Your pet personality is GIRLY FISH! You are artistic, creative and friendly. Just like Girly Fish, you keep busy by doing different hobbies and creating things. You have a real eye for colours and have your own style.

Beach

Mostly orange

Your pet personality is TIGER! You are fun, exciting and daring! Just like Tiger, you love going on adventures and trying new things. You love to push the limits and be brave! Your friends admire your non-stop energy!

Add up how many of each colour you have chosen to discover your pet personality!

Puppy Puzzles!

Help the puppies solve all of these puzzles!

1

Help the three puppies answer the questions below by drawing a circle around the correct answers.

1. What type of dog is Jackie?
   A. Labrador
   B. Beagle
   C. Corgi

2. What colour is Clancy's rope toy?
   A. green
   B. blue
   C. red

3. Which family are asleep?
   A. Beagles
   B. Labradors
   C. Retrievers

4. How many puppies are wearing nappies?
   A. 6
   B. 2
   C. 8

2

How many of Maxwell's bones can you count on these pages?

Write your answer in the box.

3

Help Jackie through the shape trail so she can be with her puppies! You can only move to the next shape if it is the same shape OR colour. Move up, down, left or right.

Start

Finish

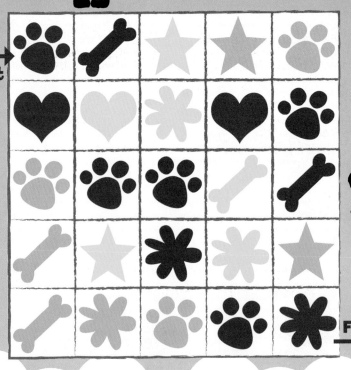

4

Use your colouring pencils to complete this pattern.

5

Read the sentences below and circle T for True or F for False.

T The Labradors' blanket is blue. **F**

T Clancy's kennel is pink. **F**

T Jackie has three puppies. **F**

6

Finish the puzzle by drawing the missing shapes in the boxes. Each shape can only appear once in each row or column.

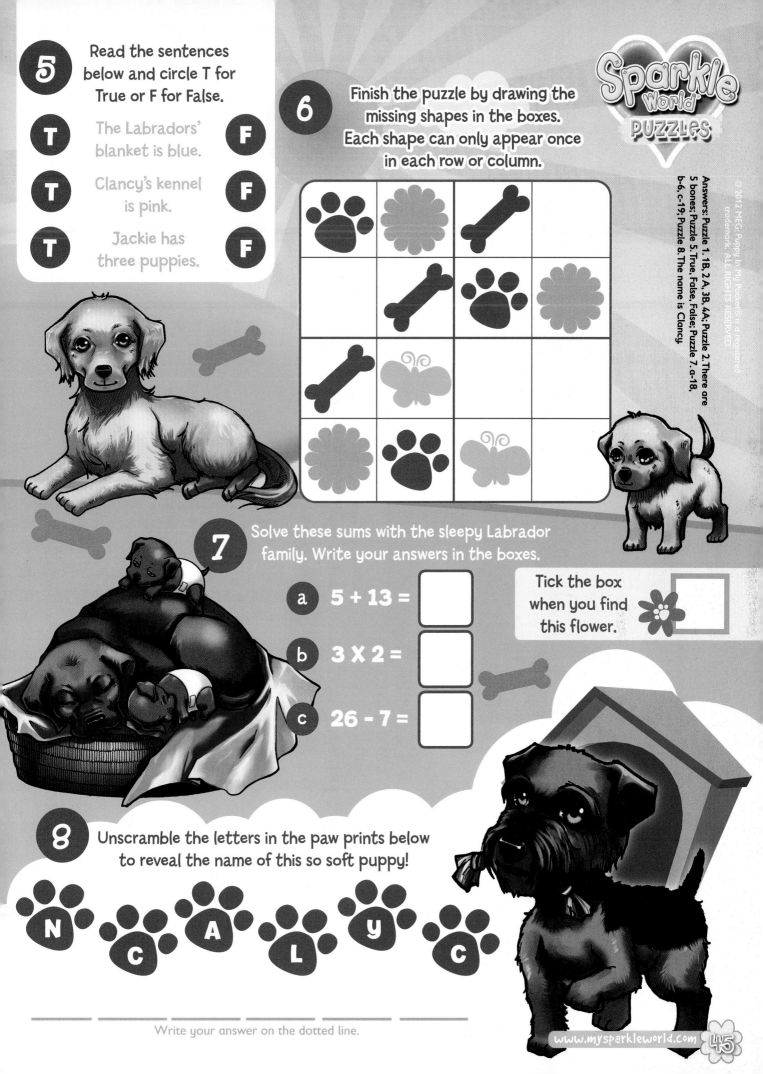

7

Solve these sums with the sleepy Labrador family. Write your answers in the boxes.

a **5 + 13 =**

b **3 X 2 =**

c **26 - 7 =**

Tick the box when you find this flower.

8

Unscramble the letters in the paw prints below to reveal the name of this so soft puppy!

N C A L y C

Write your answer on the dotted line.

Barbie's dreams come true, but should she have been careful what she wished for?

Barbie dreamed of owning her own café so she thought her dreams were beginning to come true when Teresa's mother asked her to look after her café for the day. Barbie was busy whipping up a batch of pancakes, when the first customers came in, tempted by the cakes in the window!

"Mmm, pancakes!" grinned Chelsea, running into the kitchen. "Can I have a go?"

"Sorry, not right now, Chelsea," smiled Barbie. "The café is filling up. I promise I'll teach you later!"

Chelsea was disappointed. A moment later, Skipper called in, carrying her guitar.

"Hey, Barbie, want to hear my new song?" she said, eagerly.

"I'd love to but I don't have time," said Barbie, flipping a pancake. As she did, a clap of thunder made her jump.

SPLAT! The pancake landed on the floor in a gooey heap. Chelsea giggled.

Just then Stacie hurried in.

"Hi! There's a storm heading this way," she said, shaking her umbrella. "People will need to shelter from the rain. Barbie, you're in for a crazy day!"

"This day isn't going quite the way I'd planned!" sighed Barbie. "I've a feeling I need to be four Barbies at once to get everything done!"

Skipper, Stacie and Chelsea looked at each other and they both tiptoed out. Barbie scraped up the splattered pancake, wearily, and began making a fresh one. Through the swing doors she could hear the café getting busier. Stacie was right. Everyone wanted to get in the café and out of the rain!

Barbie slid the fluffy pancake on to a plate. She topped it with fresh fruit and syrup and turned away to put the syrup jug down. When she turned back, the pancakes had gone!

"Oh, no! Where did they go?" cried Barbie, puzzled. Then she noticed the kitchen door was swinging shut. Someone had stolen them!

Barbie pushed open the door to the café and blinked in amazement. Chelsea was serving up the pancakes to a waiting customer, who looked delighted. Stacie was taking new orders and, not only that, Skipper was going around singing her new song as she poured out coffee! The customers were tapping their feet and smiling!

"I guess I don't need four Barbies after all," thought Barbie with a smile. "I just need my sisters!"

Stacie barged into the kitchen.

"We need two fried eggs and juice on table four," she yelled.

"I'm on it!" grinned Barbie.

With Stacie taking orders, Chelsea waitressing and Skipper entertaining, the day was a roaring success!

At last the storm blew over and the sun soon came out.

"Skipper, you were awesome! I love your new song," smiled Barbie as she closed the door at the end of the day. "Chelsea, Stacie, what would I have done without you? Now there are just four more customers..."

"Huh? Where?" asked Chelsea, looking around.

"She means us!" grinned Skipper, giving her a nudge.

"That's right!" laughed Barbie, and she winked at Skipper. "I'm really tired of making pancakes today though. Anyone else want to have a go?"

"Me, me!" squealed Chelsea, jumping up and down. "Ooh! I've always wanted to say this... I'M ON IT!"

SYRUP

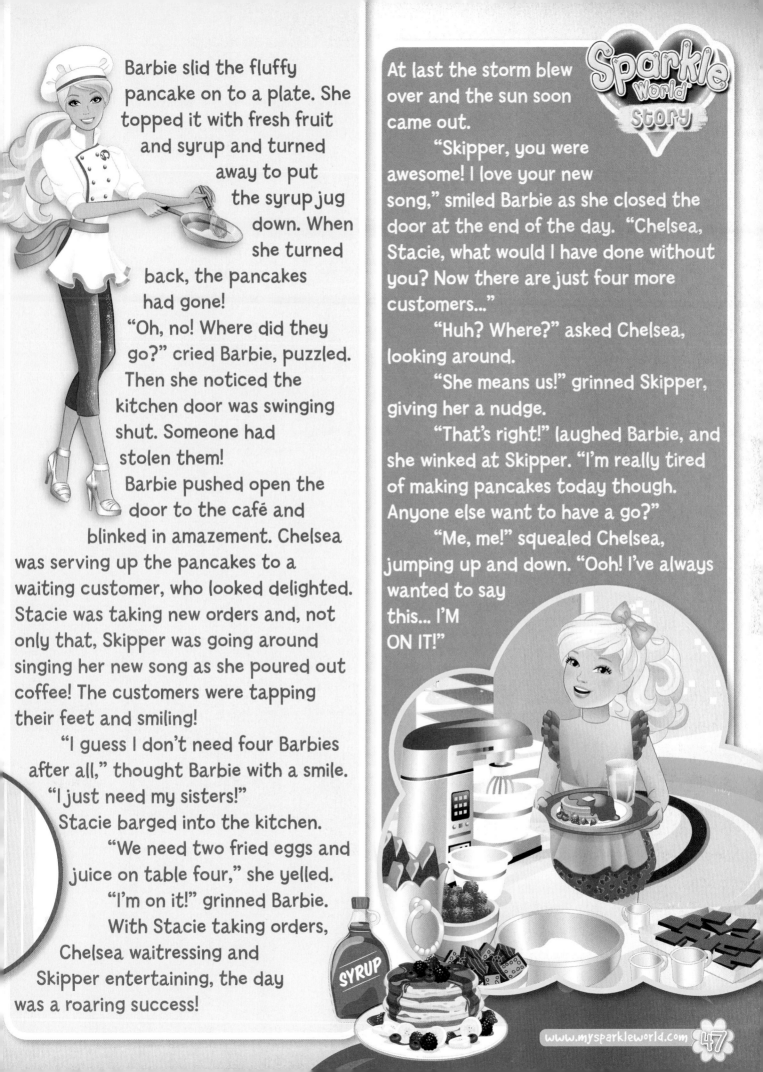

RAINBOW magic®

About Me!

The Princess Fairies want to find out all about you!
Turn these pages into your very own 'about me' profile.
Fill in the gaps and stick photos in the special spaces!

About me

Demi would like to know...

Name: ....

Birthday: ....

Home town: ....

Stick a picture
of you here!

My best friend is

Elisa would like
to see your best friend!
Stick a photo of
you both here!

....
Write their name
on the line.

A few of my favourite things.

My favourite
band: ....

My favourite
film: ....

My favourite
food: ....

My favourite
subject at
school: ....

My lucky
number is...

Write your answer in the box.

Anya would like to see a picture of your cute pets or your favourite animal!

Stick a picture of your pet or favourite animal here!

So cute!

Honor would like to know about your happiest memory!

Write about it in the space below.

....
....
....
....

Maddie would like to find out about your personality. Circle the words that best describe you!

I am...
shy   fun   happy
friendly   nervous   quiet
        kind   confident
honest
        fashionable

Colour the flower in your favourite colour.

Strawberry Shortcake™

Berry Big Wordsearch!

Help Strawberry find the words below in the wordsearch opposite. Draw a line through each word as you find it. Then colour the strawberry next to each word in the list.

STRAWBERRY

CUSTARD

PUPCAKE

LEMON

ORANGE

BERRYKIN

PLUM

FRIENDS

PUDDING

Pupcake has hidden a word in the grid opposite. Write the green letters in order in the white circles below to spell the word.

Write your answer in the circles.

How
many?

Write the numbers
in the boxes.

Sparkle
World
WORDSEARCH

B	O	R	A	N	G	E	S	K	M
H	U	P	W	O	B	R	T	L	F
L	E	M	O	N	E	M	R	P	R
A	T	S	L	E	R	O	A	U	I
I	H	C	A	W	R	V	W	D	E
N	L	I	G	N	Y	R	B	D	N
P	U	P	C	A	K	E	E	I	D
F	R	E	B	O	I	T	R	N	S
W	P	L	U	M	N	L	R	G	O
C	U	S	T	A	R	D	Y	D	S

COOKIE
JAR
CPLG AMERICAN GREETINGS

Polar Bear's Memory Game!

Test your memory skills with Polar Bear in this cool game. Good luck!

Player 1

 1

 2

3

 4

5

 6

7

 8

9

You will need: 2 players, 2 pens and 18 circles of card to cover all of the pictures below.
How to play: Cover all of the pictures with the circles of card. Take it in turns to uncover one picture from each page. If the pictures match, keep the pieces of card and colour a heart, then have another go! If the pictures don't match, cover them over again, then the other player takes their turn. The first player to colour all of their hearts is the winner.

Player 2

1
2
3
4
5
6
7
8
9

Polly Pocket — Popcorn Panic!

Kerstie

Shani

Polly

carousel

Rick

popcorn

, , and were at the amusement park. "Wheee!" they all squealed as they whirled around on the . "That was awesome," grinned afterwards. "Now all we need is to make it the best time ever," said . But when they got to the machine it wasn't working!

"Leave it to me!" said . "I never met a gadget I couldn't fix!" "Umm, maybe you shouldn't..." warned . But wasn't listening. She opened up the machine door and tweaked at something inside.

Read the story. When you see a picture, say the word instead.

How many?

Sparkle World Story

Suddenly, began to pop out in all directions. "Whoa!" yelled , ducking

as sweet whizzed past him. "Quick, catch it!" yelled handing out

boxes. 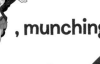 , 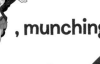 and all ran around catching it and soon they were

surrounded by a mountain of . At last the machine ran out. "What are we

going to do with all this ?" panted . "There's only one way out of this,"

laughed 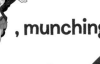 getting out her phone. "We're going to need more friends to

help us eat our way out!" "I'll be making a start!"

grinned , munching

a mouthful of .

"Now this is what I call

the best time ever!"

Barbie i can be...

Cute Cakes Bakery!

Use your crayons to colour these pictures of Barbie and Chelsea. Then try the activity at the bottom of the page.

Put a tick in the box when you find Barbie's bakes in the picture!

Strawberry's Berry Perfect Adventures!

Take Strawberry and friends' quiz to discover which adventure would suit you best. Circle your answer for each question.

Strawberry would like to know...

What do you like doing at the weekend?

A. Going to the park.

B. Dancing and playing music.

C. Going for long walks in the countryside.

Blueberry would like to know...

What would be your ideal summer holiday?

A. A busy adventure holiday.

B. A relaxing beach holiday.

C. Somewhere with new places to explore.

Raspberry would like to know...

What would be your perfect party outfit?

A. Jeans with a funky top.

B. A sparkly dress.

C. Creating a new look with my older clothes.

Sparkle World Quiz

Lemon would like to know...

Which of these jobs would you enjoy?

A. Vet or Zoo Keeper.

B. Fashion Designer.

C. Doctor or Scientist.

Orange would like to know...

What would be your perfect birthday celebration?

A. Going horse riding.

B. A shopping trip with my friends.

C. Singing karaoke tunes at a party.

Mostly As
You love adventures and keeping busy like Strawberry! Make a picnic and take your berry best friends on a walk to the park or go for a bike ride!

Mostly Bs
You love shopping and fashion like Orange! Organise a fashion day with your friends! Customise some old clothes and give each other makeovers!

Mostly Cs
You love being outside like Raspberry! See how many plants and minibeasts you can find in the park or garden and make a scrapbook of your findings!

Sparkle World crafts & recipes!

Let's have a... Princess Tea Party!

Invite your friends for a Princess Tea Party any day of the year!

Sew the bunting triangles on to the cotton ribbon!

Let's make... Bunting

You will need: Scrap material, pinking scissors, cotton bunting ribbon and a needle & cotton

What to do:
Cut out triangles of scrap material using pinking scissors so the material does not fray.
Fold the cotton bunting ribbon in half so you can put the triangles into the centre.
Sew the ribbon either side of the top of the triangles as shown in the picture.

Arrange some flowers in a teapot!

Etiquette

Good behaviour is essential at every princess tea party. Here are our top tips:

1. Place your napkin on your lap. Don't tuck it under your chin!

2. Remember your manners! Don't forget to say, please, thank you and may I.

3. Wait until everyone is served before you start eating, unless you have been told you may start.

4. Savouries should be eaten first, then scones and then sweets. Remember to chew like you have a secret!

5. Tea should be poured first and milk and sugar should be added afterwards.

6. The handle of your teacup should be held between your thumb and forefinger but don't raise your pinky!

7. Don't make slurping noises when you drink!

8. Don't dunk biscuits.

Let's make...
Strawberries and Cream Sponge

Ask an adult to preheat the oven to 180°C or gas mark 4.

Ingredients:
4 medium eggs
150g caster sugar
150g self-raising flour

To decorate:
1 punnet strawberries
150ml whipped cream

1. Grease two baking tins.
2. Break the eggs into a bowl and whisk them together lightly.
3. Add the sugar and whisk until the mixture is thick and creamy.
4. Sieve the flour into the bowl and gently fold it into the mixture.
5. Divide the mixture equally between the two tins and bake them for 25 minutes.
6. When they are cool, spread the bottom layer with whipped cream, add sliced strawberries and sprinkle some sugar on the top. Delicious!

Make your cake in shaped tins and display it on a pretty cake stand!

Fill your finger sandwiches with cream cheese and cucumber, tuna, salmon or egg and cress.

Dress up in boas, beads, rings and tiaras!

Serve your special cupcakes in a teacup and saucer!

Princess Tea Party Ideas

Here are some Princess Tea Party ideas to get you started:

1. Download your Princess Tea Party invites, place cards, menu and thank you cards from www.mysparkleworld.com.
2. Wear your hair in a traditional style and wear a pretty dress.
3. If possible, use a tea set. If you haven't got one, you may be able to borrow one or find a cheap one in a charity shop or antiques market.
4. Scatter rose petals on your table.
5. Play soothing songs at your party such as music from The Nutcracker, Swan Lake and Vivaldi or try old time tea dance music.
6. Serve elderflower cordial or pink lemonade to your guests.
7. Play some traditional party games such as Pin the Tail on the Donkey, Chinese Whispers, Squeak Piggy Squeak and Simon Says. Visit www.mysparkleworld.com for more ideas!

my Sparkle World .com

Polly's Playtime!

You will need: A dice and a counter for each player.
How to play: Take it in turns to roll the dice and move forward the number of places shown. Follow the instructions on the squares to move up or down the board. The winner is the first person to reach the finish.

41

 Scoot down to 37! **42**

43

44

45 Roll again!

Go back 2 spaces! **40**

39

38

37

Cartwheel down to 24! **36**

21

22 Miss a go!

Walk the dog. Go up to 38! **23**

24

25

Roll again! **20**

Lea has lost her football. Go down to 3! **19**

18

17

Stroke the cat. Miss a go! **16**

1 **Start**

2

3 You catch Lea's football. Miss a go!

Skate up to 17! **4**

5

Sparkle World game
Fabtastic! You made it!
46 Sing your way down to 34!
47
48
49
50 Finish
35
34
Go with Kerstie to 39! 33
32
31
26 Go forward to 29!
27
28
29
30 Skateboard down to 12!
15
14
Dance up to 29! 13
12
11
6
7 Drive up to 27!
8
9
Tell your best joke! 10

Barbie
i can be...

What's your Barbie popstar name?

Using your initials and the list below, find out your Barbie popstar name! You can also work out all of your friends' names too!

A - Adele	**N** - Nina
B - Bex	**O** - Opal
C - Ciara	**P** - Pixie
D - Delta	**Q** - Queenie
E - Electra	**R** - Riri
F - Florence	**S** - Sparkle
G - Glitter	**T** - Tia
H - Hermoine	**U** - Una
I - Indi	**V** - Valentine
J - Jessie	**W** - Willow
K - Keira	**X** - Xena
L - Lulu	**Y** - Yasmin
M - Macy	**Z** - Zen

© 2012 Mattel

How many bows can you count on this page?
Write your answer in the box below.

My Barbie popstar name is...

1. A film crew had come to Wetherbury! Kirsty and Rachel were thrilled to have got parts as fairies in a film called **The Starlight Chronicles.** "I can't wait to try out our costumes!" said Kirsty. This was perfect! The two girls had secretly been friends with real fairies for some time. They had often helped the fairies to stop Jack Frost and his goblins from causing mischief.

2. Suddenly, the actors all began getting their lines mixed up. Something was wrong! Then Kirsty spotted someone with warty green feet. "It's a goblin!" she gasped. "Follow him!"

3. As they dashed after him, Keira the Film Star Fairy burst out of some costumes. "The goblin has stolen my silver film script," she said. "It makes sure actors get their lines right!"

4. The girls could hear the goblins. They were trying to read the silver script! It gave Rachel an idea. "We need to look like Hollywood talent spotters!" she said. Keira sprinkled fairy dust and transformed their outfits into suits.

5. Keira hid in Kirsty's pocket as they went up to the goblins. "We're working on the movie," said Rachel. "We heard your performance and thought you might like a few tips." "I suppose we could do with a little help," said a goblin.

6. He handed her the silver script and at once Keira burst out of Kirsty's pocket. She tapped it with her wand, magically shrinking it down to fairy-size. "This is going back to Fairyland!" she told the goblins. "Where it belongs!"

7. Kirsty and Rachel went back to rehearsal to find everything in chaos! Keira returned from Fairyland looking worried. "Jack Frost snatched my magical megaphone!" she explained. "Without it, the director won't get everyone organised!"

8. Keira needed the girls' help! She transformed them into fairies and took them to Jack Frost's Ice Castle. He was using the megaphone to shout at the goblins. "All you had to do was bring back the silver script!" he bellowed.

9. With a wave of her wand, Keira gave everyone earplugs. Even the goblins! Jack Frost peered at the megaphone, puzzled that no one could hear him. Quick as a flash, Rachel darted in the other end, making him jump!

10. At once, Keira snatched the megaphone and it shrank to fairy-size. "Pesky fairies! Come back!" fumed Jack Frost as the fairies flew away. "Time to go!" grinned Keira. She waved her wand and whisked the girls back to their own world.

11. It was time for Kirsty and Rachel's scene with the film star. They put on their costumes, ready to start. But suddenly, all the cameras stopped working! Everyone took a break while the puzzled film crew went off to find more cameras.

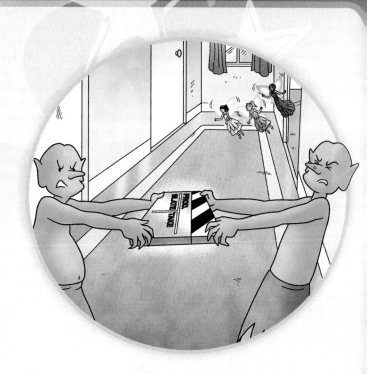

12. Just then, the girls saw a camera begin to shimmer and Keira whooshed out! "The goblins have stolen my enchanted clapperboard!" she cried. "It makes sure that filming always goes to plan. Without it the film will be a disaster!"

13. Kirsty heard a squawking giggle outside the door. "That sounded like a goblin!" she cried. Quickly, Keira turned the girls into fairies! They followed the giggles and found two goblins playing tug-of-war with the clapperboard!

14. At that moment, the goblins lost their balance and the enchanted clapperboard fell to the floor. "This is our chance!" said Rachel. Keira swooped and shrank it to fairy-size. "Got it!" she cried. "Now filming can get back to normal!"

15. "It's time for your scene," smiled Keira, making the girls human-size. "Our big moment has arrived at last!" smiled Rachel. They took their places in time to hear the director say some truly magical words, "Lights! Camera! Action!"

Kate and Magic!

Colour the picture using the small picture to help you.

MAGIC

Kate

Look carefully, how many paw prints can you count on Magic's collar?

Write your answer in the box.

The Perfect Pony Party

Twilight Sparkle is going to Pinkie Pie's party. Follow the path to show Twilight the way. Remember to collect all of the party food on the way as well as the special flowers.

K

P

E

Start

The special flowers have a letter in them. Write the matching coloured letters in the correct circles to reveal a secret word.

C

How many lollipops did Twilight Sparkle collect?

Write your answer in the box.

Sparkle World maze

A

C

U

Finish

Berry Sweet Steps!

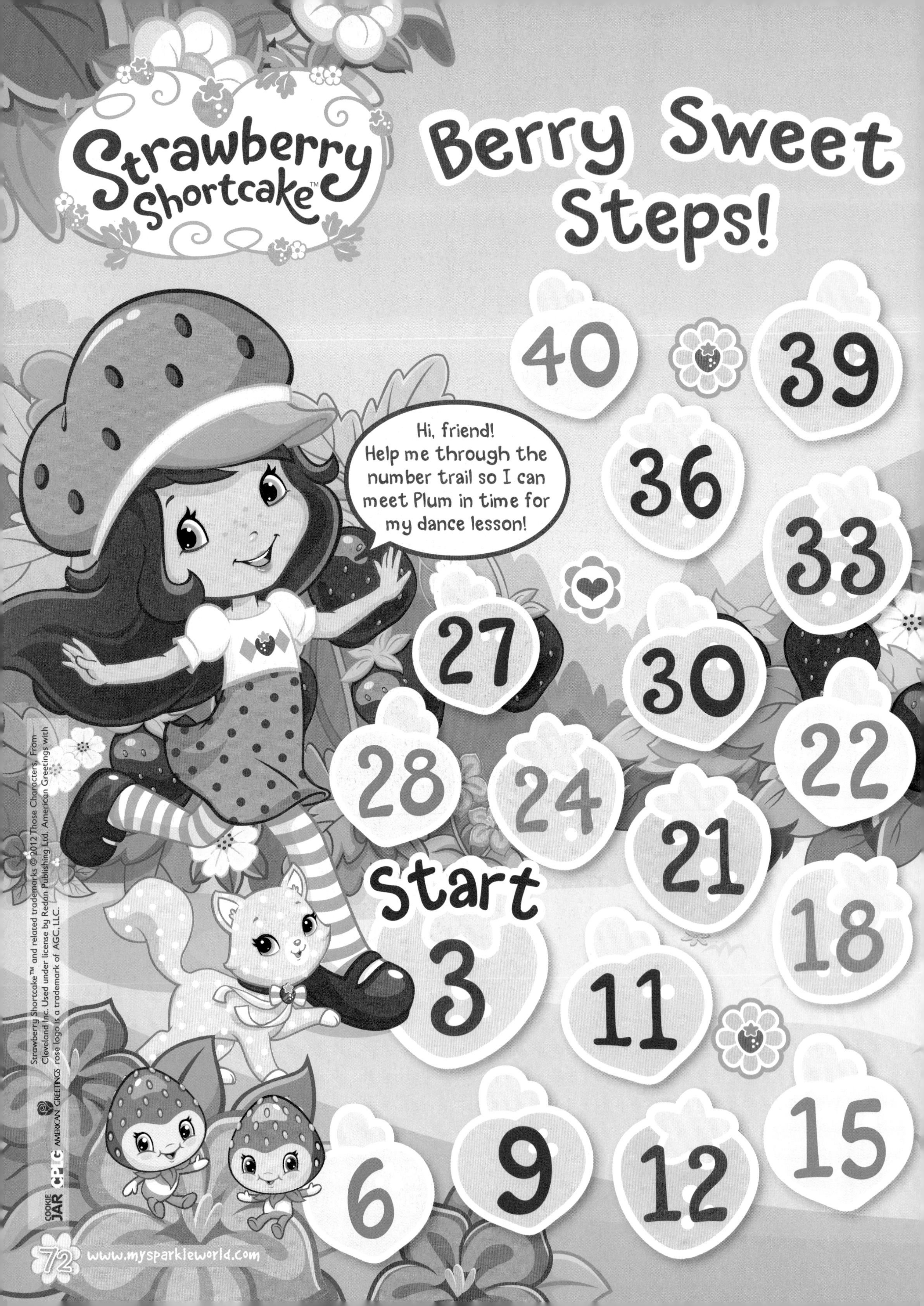

Sparkle World crafts & recipes!

Let's make Cute Canvas Shoes!

Get creative with Louise and customise your canvas shoes!

A Parent and Child Activity

You will need:
A pair of canvas shoes
fabric paints
paintbrush
An adult to help you

1 Cover your work surface with newspaper and take the laces out of your shoes. This will make it a bit easier to paint them.

2 Draw some designs on to paper. When you have decided on your fab design, pencil them on to your shoes.

3 Now get creative and paint your shoes with colourful fabric paints!

Try a pretty butterfly design!

Lou chose to paint her shoes with a cute bunny design!

Polly's Poptastic Jokes!

Sparkle World JOKES

Where can you play a rubber guitar?
In an elastic band!

What do bees sing when it's wet outside?
Stinging in the rain!

What music do balloons hate?
Pop!

What is the most dangerous kind of dancer?
A break dancer!

What is a rabbit's favourite music?
Hip-Hop!

What kind of pets sing?
Trumpets!

How do you make a bandstand?
Take their chairs away!

Why are pianos good at opening doors?
They have lots of different keys!

Puppy in my Pocket®

Adventures in Pocketville

A Puppy to love!

One day, a sparkling beam of friendship arrived over Pocketville, landing in the magical fountain. An image of a sad girl appeared in the water. The girl was in need of a friend. It was time for Princess Ava to use her magic Friendship Heart to send her a puppy. The puppies gathered around hoping to be chosen.

"I wonder who'll be the lucky puppy?" said a German Shepherd, hopefully. Princess Ava went up to a little Dalmatian.

"Little Dalmatian, I have chosen you to be the girl's special friend," she smiled.

Delighted, the Dalmatian climbed on to the enchanted fountain. The Friendship Heart glided from the Princess's collar to the fountain and with a flash of magic, sent the Dalmatian to the girl's home. The animals smiled.

Although he was happy for the lucky Dalmatian, the German Shepherd wondered if his turn would ever come. But not all the animals were happy. Princess Ava's wicked sister, Eva, was plotting.

"We'll steal the Friendship Heart tomorrow and I will be the princess!" she hissed to her friends, Zul and Gort.

The next day, the beam of friendship appeared again and another girl could be seen in the water. This time the chosen puppy was the German Shepherd!

But as the Friendship Heart glided to the fountain, Eva sent Zul leaping into action to capture it!

Princess Ava, pushed the German Shepherd to safety but as she did, Zul caught the heart in his teeth, breaking it in two! There was a magical flash and Princess Ava vanished, leaving behind her golden collar and half the heart. Eva, Zul and Gort quickly ran off with the other half. Their plan had failed!

The puppies gasped! The water from the fountain had vanished and the little girl, Kate, had magically appeared!

Find out how our Pocketville heroes, Kate and Magic, first met in this endearing tale.

Sparkle World story

"Where am I?" Kate wondered. The German Shepherd gave the magical golden collar to Kate so she could understand the animals and they explained what had happened.

"I'm your special friend. I was supposed to come to you!" said the German Shepherd. "I've always wanted a puppy!" cried Kate.

"You can choose my name!" smiled the puppy. "So many magical things have happened today!" Kate said, thoughtfully. "So, I'll call you Magic!"

"It's perfect!" laughed Magic.

"How will I get home?" Kate sighed.

"With the piece of Friendship Heart!" said William, a Royal Guard. "The Friendship Heart can make a wish come true, as long as it is shared by true friends."

"Magic and I will help find Princess Ava and we'll come back with the heart whenever you need us, so it may do its special work." Kate promised.

Kate and Magic looked at each other and made their wishes.

"My puppy and I forever together, that's all I want," said Kate.

"Kate and I forever together, that's all I want!" said Magic.

The piece of heart glimmered and Kate and Magic found themselves at Kate's.

"Look, there's Dad! And that's our house!" cried Kate. "You'll love it here!" Magic wagged his tail happily!

RAINBOW magic®

Spot the Differences!

Look carefully at the two pictures below. Can you find 8 differences in picture B? Circle the differences as you find them.

A

How many balloons can you count?

Write the answer in the box.

Circle the odd one out.

A.

B.

C.

D.

Can you spot the hidden cherries?

B

Answers: 1. The bee has disappeared; 2. Sienna has lost her wand; 3. A green vine has appeared on the castle; 4. A turret is missing on the castle; 5. A green balloon has appeared; 6. A window is now yellow; 7. A cloud under the rainbow has disappeared; 8. The castle door is missing.

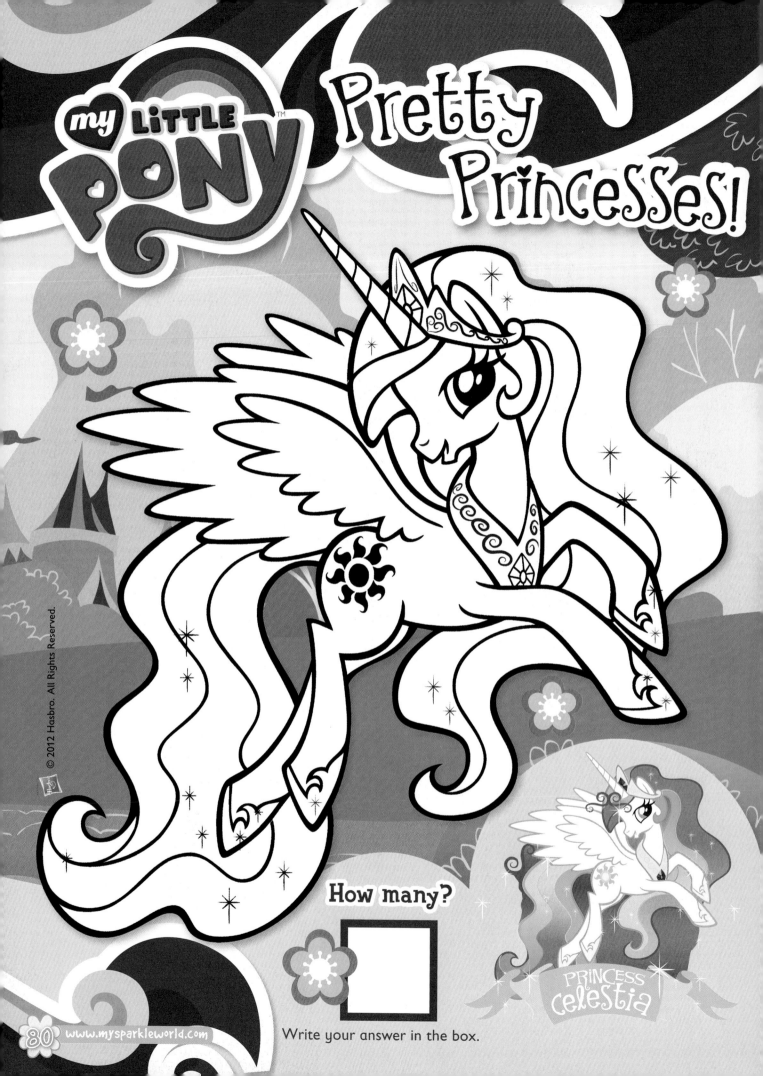

My Little Pony™

Pretty Princesses!

How many?

Write your answer in the box.

PRINCESS Celestia

YooHoo & Friends™

Best Friend Quiz!

Sit opposite your friend with the Sparkle World Annual between you. With a pencil, answer the questions by colouring the flower by your answer. Turn the Annual round and count how many answers your friend got right. Then check your friendship score.

My friend's favourite colour is...

Her favourite YooHoo and Friends character is...

Her favourite treat is...

The thing we most love to do together is...

Bake cakes Ride our bikes Dance

When she grows up, she would like to be a...

Fashion designer  Vet Scientist

When she grows up, she would like to be a...

✿ Fashion designer   ✿ Vet   ✿ Scientist

The thing we most love to do together is...

✿ Bake cakes   ✿ Ride our bikes   ✿ Dance

Her favourite treat is ...

Her favourite YooHoo and Friends character is...

My friend's favourite colour is ...

Your friendship score!

0-2

You still have lots of things to find out about each other.
Pammee's Tip: Have a sleepover party! You'll soon know everything about each other!

3-4

You know each other's secrets, but also have a big circle of friends.
Pammee's Tip: Make friendship bracelets for each other, to show your friend how much you care!

5

You are true besties! You love hanging out and have lots of fun.
Pammee's Tip: Join a club together. You'll find out new things about each other!

Monster in the Sea!

Read the story below. When you see a picture, say the word instead!

Picture key:
- Sun
- Boy Monkey
- Sea
- Cat
- Seal
- chair
- Fish
- Sea Turtle

The [Sun] was shining on Littlest Pet Shop Beach. [Cat] and [Boy Monkey] scampered on to the sand, ready for fun! "Oh, no!" said [Boy Monkey]. "I wanted to go surfing in the [Sea], but there's no one on the lifeguard [chair]." "I'll be the lifeguard," said [Cat]. "Okay! Watch out for [Sea] monsters," joked [Boy Monkey], dashing into the waves. [Cat] leapt up on to the tall [chair] to watch for danger. "I hope [Sea] monsters aren't real!" thought [Cat]. Suddenly, [Cat] spotted a strange creature in the [Sea]. It had a green head, a purple body and a blue tail! "Wow, there really is a [Sea] monster!" shouted [Cat]. "[Boy Monkey], come out of the [Sea] at once!" "Help!" cried [Boy Monkey] quickly swimming for the beach. Just then, the green head, purple body and blue tail popped up out of the water. But it wasn't a monster at all. It was

Whose head popped
out of the water?
Draw a circle around
the correct pet.

Sparkle
World
story

really ,  and  all going for a swim together. "Sorry, ,"

sighed . "I guess I'm not a very good lifeguard." "Oh, yes you are!" chuckled

. "Now I know if I'm in danger, you'll be sure to warn me in time! You're the

best lifeguard ever, !"

You're
the best
lifeguard
ever!

LIFE
GUARD

L P S

TLEST PET
OP BEACH

Barbie Fab Fashion!

With the help of Barbie's friends, can you design a gorgeous outfit for her? Colour in the heart shape by your favourite thing in each box.

Which cool dress would Barbie love?

Skipper

Which sparkly bag would Barbie choose?

Nikki

Which fabtastic shoes would Barbie pick?

Chelsea

Barbie

Help me choose accessories to complete my look!

hairband

sunglasses

watch

bangles

necklace

Strawberry Shortcake™

A Berry Fun Game!

Start 1

2

Strawberry's fruit **3**

4

Finish 20

If you haven't found all of the girls' fruits, go back to the start!

We love the Berry Cafe!

19

Orange Blossom

Player 1   Player 2

18

Lemon's fruit

Cherry Jam

Player 1   Player 2

17   **16**   **15**   **14**

Help the puppies find the different dog breeds below in the wordsearch. Cross out each word in the list as you find it.

Puppy In my Pocket

Colour this bone when you find Lenny the Golden Retriever Puppy's pretty bow!

1. husky
2. airedale
3. corgi
4. beagle
5. poodle
6. collie
7. bulldog
8. lurcher
9. pug
10. boxer

b	a	o	d	p	b	c	o
u	i	l	p	o	e	o	b
l	r	u	u	o	a	r	o
l	e	r	g	d	g	g	x
d	d	c	o	l	l	i	e
o	a	h	a	e	e	b	r
g	l	e	h	u	s	k	y
x	e	r	d	l	e	i	

YooHoo & Friends™

© Aurora World Corp.

The Grumpy Gorilla!

YooHoo, Pammee, Chewoo, Lemmee and Roodee were on a worldwide adventure! They had come from Yootopia in search of thirty lost green seeds that had blown from the Tree of Life.

One day, the five friends were using leaves to glide over the Congo in Africa. They had come a long way and were feeling hungry.

"Let's see if there's anything to eat around here," said YooHoo. They glided gently down to the ground and looked around, hoping to find some tasty fruit.

"I don't see any fruit!" grumbled Chewoo. "I'm so very hungry! I need some food NOW!"

"Shh, listen!" whispered Pammee, her ears pricking up. "Did anyone hear a rumbling, roaring sound?"

"It's probably Chewoo's tummy!" joked Lemmee. They all laughed!

"It wasn't me!" said Chewoo.

Everyone listened, and sure enough there was a rumbling, roaring sound. It was coming from the trees and it was getting closer.

Roodee quickly looked in his Yootopedia to find out what it might be.

"It says gorillas live around here!" he told them. "And that sounds like one too!"

"Quick, run!" yelled YooHoo. Roodee, Chewoo, Lemmee, Pammee and YooHoo all dashed through the rainforest as fast as they could run. Pammee turned and looked behind her to make sure YooHoo was keeping up. But he wasn't there!

"Where's YooHoo?" cried Pammee. "He was behind us," said Lemmee.

"Let's go back and find him," said Chewoo. "He might need our help!"

As quietly as they could, the group crept through the trees, looking for YooHoo.

"YooHoo, where are you?" hissed Roodee, rather impatiently.

"Here I am, guys!" they heard YooHoo call, cheerfully.

The four friends peeped through the leaves and gasped. YooHoo was there sitting right in front of the great big gorilla!

"I saw the gorilla was limping," explained YooHoo. "He's got thorns in his feet, that's why he was roaring! Look, here's one!" He tugged out a thorn and held it up for the others to see.

"We can help!" offered Chewoo. They all rushed forward to help pull the sharp thorns out of the gorilla's feet. When they had finished, the gorilla stood up and smiled happily.

"I think his feet feel much better now," chuckled YooHoo.

Suddenly, there was another loud rumbling noise.

"That really was my tummy this time," sighed Chewoo. "I'm so hungry!"

The gorilla grinned and climbed up into a tree. He swung from branch to branch, throwing down all different kinds of fruit.

"Hooray!" everyone cheered. And they all enjoyed a delicious lunch with their new gorilla friend.